Keto Juicing Recipes

The Best Keto Juices for Weight Loss

BY: Ivy Hope

IVY HOPE
COOKBOOK

Copyright/License Page

Table of Contents

Introduction 7

Chapter 1: Smoothies recipes 9

Berry Chocolate Smoothie 10

Strawberry Chocolate Smoothie 12

Strawberry Avocado Smoothie 14

Raspberry Almond Smoothie 16

Lemon Avocado Raspberry Smoothie 18

Delicious Raspberry Cheesecake Smoothie 20

Chia Blackberry Smoothie 22

Avocado Berry Spinach Smoothie 24

Fresh Mint Spinach Avocado Smoothie 26

Berry Cantaloupe Smoothie 28

Choco Cherry Smoothie 30

Carrot Lover Smoothie 32

Pineapple Papaya Smoothie 34

Baby Kale and Yogurt Smoothie 36

Nutty Arugula Yogurt Smoothie...38

Vanilla-Flavored Chai Smoothie...40

Raspberry-Coffee Creamy Smoothie 42

Parsley Smoothie...44

Chapter 2: Cocktails and Lemonade recipes..46

Multi Vegetables Cocktail..47

Ginger Cocktail 49

Rhubarb Cocktail...51

Rosemary Lemonade..53

Mint Lemonade 55

Ginger Lemonade..57

Raspberry Lemonade...59

Strawberry Basil Lemonade 61

Green Spinach Lemonade 63

Chapter 3: Juices recipes...65

Beets Breakfast Juice 66

Celery Kale Juice 68

Zucchini Juice 70

Radish Juice.. 72

Spinach Juice.. 74

Celery and Spinach Juice 76

Swiss Chard Juice... 78

Tomato Juice 80

Cauliflower Juice.. 82

Celery and Parsley Juice 84

Cucumber and Mint Juice 86

Bell Pepper Juice.. 88

Kale Juice 90

Winter Green Juice.. 92

Chard Parsley Green Juice 94

Mango, Strawberry, and Banana Juice........................ 96

Broccoli, Cucumber and Kiwi Juice 98

Mango and Green Tea Juice.. 100

Apple, Red Leaf Lettuce, and Cucumber Juice........... 102

Cucumber, Kale and Spinach Juice............................. 104

Sweet Potato, Bell Pepper, Beet and Carrot Juice....... 106

Asparagus, Coriander, and Onion Juice 108

Avocado, Spinach, and Lime Juice 110

Spinach, Carrot, and Watercress Juice 112

Conclusion 114

About the Author 115

Author's Afterthoughts 116

Introduction

Okay, so you've gone keto. Do you know that high fat, high protein, low-carb foods that are all the rage? Yeah, that's keto. But one thing many people overlook when they go keto is nutrition in liquid form. Luckily this is where juicing comes in! Juicing offers a quick and easy way to get your fill of fruits and vegetables with minimal prep time or dishes to clean up afterward.

But, even if you're juicing for health and not specifically keto, there are still some things you will want to keep in mind. You might be surprised to learn that the sugar content can vary significantly from fruit to fruit! Even though a piece of fruit is mostly fructose, this doesn't mean it's healthier than a piece of kale or cabbage. So we highly recommend consulting nutrition charts for each vegetable before purchase.

The best juicing recipes for keto include fruits that are high in water content, such as cucumber. This helps prevent stomach bloating since you're not taking in a lot of fiber to fill your belly.

Happy juicing!

Chapter 1: Smoothies recipes

Berry Chocolate Smoothie

A lot of people, myself included, enjoy a good Smoothie as an easy and healthy breakfast. The Berry Chocolate Smoothie recipe I have for you is perfect for any time of day! It is made with frozen berries for a pleasantly cool sensation on your tongue and can easily be made ahead of time! So what are you waiting for? You're going to love this smoothie!

Prep Time: 5 minutes

Serves: 2

Ingredients:

- ¾ cup frozen mixed berries
- ¼ cup heavy whipping cream
- ¾ tsp. vanilla
- 1 packet stevia
- 2 tbsp. unsweetened cocoa powder
- 2 tbsp. almonds
- ½ avocado
- Pinch of salt

Instructions:

1. Add all ingredients into the blender and blend until smooth and well combined.

2. Serve immediately and enjoy.

Strawberry Chocolate Smoothie

What do you get when you take fruit, a chocolate-covered fruit, and some milk? A strawberry chocolate smoothie! This is a perfect summer drink for eating and drinking with your hands. And it's healthy too!

It's that simple to make this quick, cool summertime drink.

Prep Time: 5 minutes

Serves: 1

Ingredients:

- ½ tsp. cocoa nibs
- ½ cup frozen strawberries
- ½ avocado
- 1 scoop collagen protein
- 1 scoop chocolate protein powder

Instructions:

1. Add all ingredients into the blender and blend until smooth and creamy.

2. Serve immediately and enjoy.

Strawberry Avocado Smoothie

Do you enjoy the taste of strawberries and avocados? Maybe you want a healthy breakfast or a light meal? If this sounds like what you're looking for, then this smoothie will be perfect for you. It's delicious, healthy, easy to make, and proud of its reasonably short ingredient list. This recipe is vegan with no added sugars.

Prep Time: 5 minutes

Serves: 2

Ingredients:

- ½ tsp. vanilla extract
- 1 ½ cups unsweetened almond milk
- 1 tbsp. cocoa powder
- 1 avocado, chopped
- 1 cup frozen strawberries

Instructions:

1. Add all ingredients into the blender and blend until smooth and creamy.

2. Serve immediately and enjoy.

Raspberry Almond Smoothie

You know that fruit is good for your health, but it can be difficult to incorporate enough into your diet. Smoothies offer a convenient way to amp up the fruit quotient in just one glass, and they're quick and easy to make.

Prep Time: 5 minutes

Serves: 2

Ingredients:

- ½ cup unsweetened almond milk
- 20 almonds
- ½ cup raspberries
- 4 oz. yogurt

Instructions:

1. Add all ingredients into the blender and blend until smooth and creamy.

2. Serve immediately and enjoy.

Lemon Avocado Raspberry Smoothie

I love this refreshing smoothie! It is light yet satisfying and has a delicious citrus taste. I prefer it over coffee because it is low in caffeine. Plus, the ingredients are very affordable and easy to find at your local grocery store. If you want a more protein-packed version, add some Greek yogurt or protein powder.

Prep Time: 5 minutes

Serves: 2

Ingredients:

- 3 tbsp. fresh lemon juice
- ½ cup raspberries, frozen
- 1 1/3 cup of water
- 1 avocado
- 1 tbsp. swerve

Instructions:

1. Combine all ingredients in the blender and process until smooth and creamy.

2. Serve immediately and enjoy.

Delicious Raspberry Cheesecake Smoothie

This smoothie is a refreshing, light dessert that's easy to make and almost impossible to resist! The raspberry cheesecake smoothie is made with fresh raspberries, cinnamon applesauce, and vanilla yogurt...and yes–almond milk too. If you're looking for a healthy and fun way to spice up your day, this smoothie recipe is it.

Prep Time: 5 minutes

Serves: 2

Ingredients:

- 2 cups ice cubes
- 1 ½ tsp. vanilla extract
- ¼ tsp. liquid stevia
- 10 oz. raspberries
- ½ cup cottage cheese
- 1 cup coconut water

Instructions:

1. Add all ingredients into the blender and blend until smooth and creamy.

2. Serve immediately and enjoy.

Chia Blackberry Smoothie

You can't beat summer without a healthy breakfast, and this Chia Blackberry Smoothie recipe is just the ticket! This blackberry smoothie has chia seeds to boost protein as well as antioxidants, vitamins, and minerals. You will need to allow it to chill in the fridge overnight, but that means you get an extra dose of that refreshing cold blueberry flavor.

Prep Time: 5 minutes

Serves: 2

Ingredients:

- ½ cup ice cubes
- ¾ cup water
- 1 scoop vanilla protein powder
- ½ tsp. vanilla extract
- 1/8 cup almonds
- ½ tsp. ground cinnamon
- 1 tbsp. chia seeds
- ¾ cup blackberries

Instructions:

1. Add all ingredients into the blender and blend until smooth and creamy.

2. Serve immediately and enjoy.

Avocado Berry Spinach Smoothie

Avocado Berry Spinach Smoothie is a refreshing, healthy, and easy-to-make breakfast recipe. It's a great way to start your day if you're trying to eat more greens! Avocado and spinach are excellent sources of plant-based protein and calcium. This smoothie tastes like summer in an 8 oz glass!

This recipe is straightforward, making it ideal for the beginner cook or berry novice.

Prep Time: 10 minutes

Serves: 1

Ingredients:

- 5 drops liquid stevia
- 1 tsp. vanilla extract
- 5 basil leaves
- 1 tbsp. MCT oil
- 1 scoop collagen protein powder
- ¼ cup blueberries
- 1 tbsp. heavy cream
- ½ avocado
- 1 cup baby spinach
- 1 cup water

Instructions:

1. Add all ingredients into the blender and blend until smooth and thick.

2. Serve immediately and enjoy!

Fresh Mint Spinach Avocado Smoothie

The combination of avocado and mint is like a match made in heaven. The taste is tangy, refreshing, and clean tasting. This spinach smoothie tastes so good it can make you forget all about your calorie intake goals.

Prep Time: 5 minutes

Serves: 1

Ingredients:

- ½ cup water
- 2 tbsp. fresh lemon juice
- ½ cup fresh mint leaves
- 1 cup spinach
- ½ avocado

Instructions:

1. Add all ingredients into the blender and blend until smooth and well combined.

2. Serve and enjoy.

Berry Cantaloupe Smoothie

I love a good smoothie in the summertime. But sometimes, I want to add some protein to my meal, and this Berry Cantaloupe Smoothie is perfect for that! It's healthy and delicious so that you can feel good about it!

It also tastes amazing! And remember how refreshing it is? The added citrus from the orange balances out the cantaloupe nicely.

Prep Time: 5 minutes

Serves: 2

Ingredients:

- 1 tsp. chia seeds
- 1 cup cantaloupe, chopped
- 1 cup strawberries
- ½ cup unsweetened coconut milk

Instructions:

1. Add all ingredients into the blender and blend until smooth and creamy.

2. Serve and enjoy.

Choco Cherry Smoothie

Choco Cherry Smoothie is one of my favorite smoothies that I like to drink for breakfast because it is delicious, healthy, and easy to make.

Prep Time: 5 minutes

Serves: 2

Ingredients:

- 1 cup ice cubes
- 5 drops liquid stevia
- ¼ cup unsweetened cocoa powder
- 1/3 cup hemp hearts
- 1 scoop protein powder
- 1 cup unsweetened coconut milk
- ½ cup cherries

Instructions:

1. Add all ingredients into the blender and blend until smooth and creamy.

2. Serve immediately and enjoy.

Carrot Lover Smoothie

This recipe is a simple, delicious, healthy carrot smoothie. This is a yummy drink that is perfect for an evening dinner or a snack in the morning.

Prep Time: 5 minutes

Serves: 1

Ingredients

- ½ Banana frozen, chopped
- 8 oz. Almond milk
- 1.4 oz. frozen Strawberries
- 1.4 oz. frozen Raspberries
- 1/2 cup Vanilla syrup
- 2 oz. Carrot slices
- 2 cups walnuts, chopped

Instructions:

1. Add all of the ingredients, except the milk, to the NutriBullet before adding in the milk to the max-fill line.

2. Blend until the smoothie reaches your desired consistency.

Pineapple Papaya Smoothie

Pineapple papaya smoothie is a quick and easy breakfast recipe that uses frozen fruit, just four ingredients, and a blender. It's healthy, refreshing, and tastes delicious! So what are you waiting for? Make this now.

I hope you enjoy this delicious smoothie recipe as much as I do!

Sleepy morning? No time to eat breakfast? We have the perfect solution for your troubled day-pineapple papaya smoothie.

Prep Time: 5 minutes

Serves: 1

Ingredients

- ½ cup frozen and cubes Pineapple
- ½ cup Papaya
- ½ Banana frozen and chopped
- 8 oz. Almond milk
- 1 scoop Plain whey protein powder
- 3 tsp. Coconut oil

Instructions:

1. Add all ingredients, except the milk, to the NutriBullet before adding the milk to the max-fill line.

2. Blend until the smoothie reaches your desired consistency.

Baby Kale and Yogurt Smoothie

What a great smoothie recipe! I love the combination of the baby kale and the yogurt. This is a perfect breakfast or snack."

Though you may be skeptical at first, blending kale with yogurt makes for an amazing smoothie. The nutrients in both ingredients complement each other, making this an ideal way to start your day and fuel your body for any activity that might come up later.

Prep Time: 5 minutes

Serves: 1

Ingredients:

- 1 cup whole milk yogurt
- 1 cup baby kale greens
- 1 packet Stevia, or more to taste
- 1 tbsp. MCT oil
- 1 tbsp. sunflower seeds
- 1 cup water

Instructions:

1. Add all ingredients to the blender.

2. Blend until smooth and creamy.

3. Serve and enjoy.

Nutty Arugula Yogurt Smoothie

A fruity and creamy smoothie that is easy to make with any kind of fruit you have on hand. Enjoy this healthy drink as a breakfast or afternoon snack.

Prep Time: 5 minutes

Serves: 1

Ingredients:

- 1 cup whole milk yogurt
- 1 cup baby arugula
- 1 packet Stevia, or more to taste
- 1 tbsp. avocado oil
- 2 tbsps. macadamia nuts
- 1 cup water

Instructions:

1. Add all ingredients to the blender.

2. Blend until smooth and creamy.

3. Serve and enjoy.

Vanilla-Flavored Chai Smoothie

What's better than a hot cup of tea? A cold cup, of course!

This warm, frothy iced beverage can be made at home with just a few ingredients. If you're out and about or in a rush to prepare dinner, just pick up some non-dairy milk, vanilla frozen yogurt or ice cream, and an Indian chai tea mix like Darjeeling. Throw it all in the blender until smooth and delightfully creamy.

Prep Time: 5 minutes

Serves: 1

Ingredients:

- 1 ½ cups boiling water
- 1 black tea bag
- ¼ tsp. ginger
- ¼ tsp. cinnamon
- ¼ tsp. cardamom powder
- 2 packets Stevia or as desired
- ½ cup coconut milk
- 1 tsp. real vanilla extract
- ¼ avocado fruit

Instructions:

1. In a large mug, mix boiling water, ginger, cinnamon, and cardamom powder. Add tea bag and let it steep until liquid is cool.

2. Remove tea bag and squeeze out excess liquid and discard. Refrigerate liquid with spices until chilled. You can even transfer it to an ice cube tray and freeze it.

3. Add all ingredients to the blender.

4. Blend until smooth and creamy.

5. Serve and enjoy.

Raspberry-Coffee Creamy Smoothie

Are you looking for a concoction to perk up your mood on a dreary day? Look no further than this creamy,   healthy-for-you, caffeine-free smoothie that tastes just like coffee and raspberry. This is the perfect beverage for when you need to wake up.

Prep Time: 5 minutes

Serves: 1

Ingredients:

- ½ cup coconut milk
- 1 ½ cups brewed coffee, chilled
- ¼ cup Raspberries
- ¼ avocado fruit
- 2 packets Stevia or more to taste
- 1 tsp. chia seeds

Instructions:

1. Add all ingredients to the blender.

2. Blend until smooth and creamy.

3. Serve and enjoy.

Parsley Smoothie

Do you have some extra parsley hanging around in your kitchen? Why not try blending it up with some berries and other healthy ingredients to make a delicious smoothie? This recipe is packed with vitamin C, healthy fats, and antioxidants.

Servings: 1

Preparation time: 5 minutes

Ingredients:

- 1 orange, seeded and peeled
- 1 medium cucumber, peeled
- 1 inch piece of ginger
- ¼ cup spinach
- ¼ cup parsley
- 1 lemon, seeded and peeled
- 2 tablespoons avocado oil
- 1 cup filtered water
- 1 cup ice cubes

Instructions:

1. Prepare vegetables and rinse them thoroughly.

2. Cur orange, cucumber, ginger, and lemon into small pieces and add to a blender.

3. Add remaining ingredients and pulse at high speed for 1 to 2 minutes or until smooth.

4. Pour smoothie into a glass, then stir in oil until mixed and serve.

Chapter 2: Cocktails and Lemonade recipes

Multi Vegetables Cocktail

This stunning and delicious side dish is the perfect solution to your side dish dilemma. With just a handful of ingredients, it will have you excited about how easy it is to put this together at home. The taste? Spectacularly clean with a crisp yet creamy texture.

Prep time: 3 minutes

Serves: 2

Ingredients:

- 1 bell pepper, deseeded, cored, sliced
- 1 bunch of spinach, rinsed
- 2 cups tomato juice
- Dash of black pepper
- Dash of salt

Instructions:

1. Add all ingredients to a blender and pulse on high until smooth.

2. Serve.

Ginger Cocktail

The Ginger Cocktail is a refreshing coffee-based drink that can be served before a meal or an evening drink. It is made by pouring one shot of espresso into a ginger ale, grenadine, and simple syrup mixture. The original recipe used equal parts of ginger ale and grenadine, but the taste may vary depending on how much syrup you add.

Prep time: 3 minutes

Serves: 1

Ingredients:

- 1 cup kefir, low fat
- 2 tsp. ginger root, grated
- 1 tsp. cinnamon
- Dash of red hot pepper

Instructions:

1. Add all ingredients to a blender and pulse on high until smooth.

2. Serve.

Rhubarb Cocktail

This refreshing and tangy drink is the perfect way to cool down in the summertime. Made with rhubarb, this cocktail is surprisingly easy and fast to make for every occasion. You'll be celebrating by the pool or on a rooftop in no time!

Prep time: 3 minutes

Serves: 1-2

Ingredients:

- 1/3 whole pineapple, peeled, cored
- 2 rhubarb stalks, peeled, cut in pieces
- 1 cup orange juice
- Fresh mint leaves, to taste (2-4 leaves)

Instructions:

1. Add all ingredients to a blender and pulse on high until smooth.

2. Serve.

Rosemary Lemonade

Your eyes are probably fixed on the sugar, but did you know that lemons can provide a myriad of health benefits? Did you know that they're even good for your skin? You can enjoy both health and beauty with some lemonade!

Rosemary Lemonade is a sparkling beverage made from fresh-squeezed juice and rosemary.

Prep Time: 15 minutes + 1-2 hours to cool in the fridge

Serves: 2

Ingredients:

- 2 sprigs of rosemary
- ½ tsp. ginger
- 3 lemons, juice + zest
- 2 cups water
- 12 drops liquid stevia
- Ice, to taste (usually more than half glass-covered)

Instructions:

1. In a pan, combine water, lemon peel, and 1 rosemary sprig. Bring to boil. Then boil for 5 min.

2. Remove from heat and filter out the peel and the sprig.

3. Add ginger and let cool.

4. Stir in stevia and lemon juice.

5. Put a rosemary sprig and some lemon slices into a jar and pour the lemonade into it.

6. Cool in the fridge.

Mint Lemonade

With all the intense flavors that exist in the world, it seems a shame to drink lemonade. It's easy to mix mint and sugar with the standard recipe for a refreshing yet unusual beverage.

Prep time: 1 hour 3 minutes

Serves: 2

Ingredients:

- 2 lemons, juiced
- ½ cup fresh mint leaves, chopped
- 1 tsp. stevia, liquid
- 4 cups sparkling water

Instructions:

1. Combine all ingredients and let stand in the fridge for 1 hour.

2. Filter and serve.

Ginger Lemonade

Ginger Lemonade is a refreshing and tangy drink that is perfect for the summertime. This recipe for ginger lemonade starts with fresh ginger, lemon juice, and simple syrup (or sugar). Combined and placed in a pitcher with ice, it makes a great drink to serve at your next barbecue or dinner party. Your imagination only limits the possibilities of the ingredients! Some other variations include using blueberries or strawberries in place of lemon juice.

Prep time: 15 minutes

Serves: 1 cup

Ingredients:

- ½ cup water
- ½ cup lemon juice
- 2-inch piece ginger, peeled, sliced
- 1 tsp. liquid stevia
- Sparkling water
- Ice (usually more than half glass-covered)

Instructions:

1. In a pot, combine water, sweetener, and ginger. Bring to a boil and remove from heat and let cool.

2. Add lemon juice.

3. Strain the mixture into a jar and store it in the fridge.

4. To serve, take some lemon ginger syrup and mix with sparkling water and ice.

Raspberry Lemonade

Raspberry Lemonade is a thirst-quenching drink. This recipe combines raspberries and lemon juice to create a sweet, tangy, and tart beverage perfect for sunny days or hot summer nights. It's a refreshing drink for any occasion.

Prep time: 2 minutes

Serves: 3

Ingredients:

- 1 cup raspberry
- 1 cup lemon juice
- 3 cups water
- Ice, to taste (usually more than half glass-covered)

Instructions:

1. Blend 1 cup raspberry with 3/4 cup water.

2. Strain mixture, keeping only the liquid.

3. Combine raspberry water, lemon juice, water, and ice.

Strawberry Basil Lemonade

It's a refreshing drink that you can serve cold or hot for those who prefer something different. Strawberries and basil is an odd-sounding flavor combination that somehow just works. If you're looking for an elegant way to switch up lemonade, this is it! Also, for a fun flavor variation, try this with a sprig of fresh thyme instead of basil.

Prep Time: 5 Minutes

Serves: 1

Ingredients:

- 1 cup water
- 1 tablespoon fresh lemon juice
- 7 drops liquid stevia
- ¼ cup sliced fresh strawberries
- 3 fresh basil leaves
- ½ cup ice cubes

Instructions:

1. Add the water, lemon juice, and stevia to a glass.

2. Add the strawberries, basil, and ice. Stir.

3. Serve.

Green Spinach Lemonade

Green spinach and lemonade might not sound like two ingredients that would blend well, but don't knock it before you try it. This leafy green lemonade is so good, and you'll be making it all summer long! It's a refreshing drink that also will help with your summer body goals.

Prep Time: 5 Minutes

Serves: 1

Ingredients:

- 1 medium green apple, cored
- 4 leaves of kale, chopped
- 1 cup spinach, chopped
- 2 stalks of celery
- 1-inch piece of ginger
- 1 lemon
- 1 scoop whey protein powder
- 2 tablespoons avocado oil

Instructions:

1. Prepare vegetables and fruits and rinse them thoroughly.

2. Then cut apple and ginger into bite-size pieces.

3. Place juicer collector under the juicer's nozzle, switch it on and process all the ingredients until thoroughly juiced.

4. Pour the juice into a blender, add remaining ingredients, and pulse until smooth.

5. Pour the juice into a chilled glass and serve straight away.

Chapter 3: Juices recipes

Beets Breakfast Juice

Beets have an earthy sweetness that is enhanced by the addition of an apple. The flavor profile is bold and pure in taste, contrasting with the subtle tang of cucumber. This juice has a beautiful balance that can carry you through your morning. Packed with nutrients, it's no wonder it's the #1 selling all-natural beet juice at Whole Foods!

Beets break down into sugar during juicing and contribute a nice shot of energy to your morning.

Prep Time: 5 Minutes

Serves: 5

Ingredients:

- 1 carrot, top removed
- 2 beets, peeled and top removed
- 2 apples, seeded and cored
- 2 lemons, peeled
- 2 tablespoons avocado oil

Instructions:

1. Prepare vegetables and fruits and rinse them thoroughly.

2. Then cut a carrot and beets into long slices and cut apples into small pieces.

3. Place juicer collector under the juicer's nozzle, switch it on and process all the ingredients until thoroughly juiced.

4. Add avocado oil into prepared juice, stir well and pour into chilled glasses.

5. Serve straight away.

Celery Kale Juice

Celery Kale Juice is a juicing technique, which promotes the health benefits of fresh vegetable juice. It takes celery stalks and kale leaves and blends them with water to create a creamy carrot-celery-ginger-apple juice mix! Be sure to drink your juice immediately for the best taste.

For hundreds of years, people have been drinking homemade concoctions of powerful juices for their health benefits.

Prep Time: 5 Minutes

Serves: 1

Ingredients:

- 4 kale leaves
- 1 cup spinach leaves
- 3 medium stalks of celery
- 1 medium cucumber, peeled
- 1-inch piece of ginger, peeled
- 1 lemon, peeled, halved and seeded
- 2 tablespoons avocado oil

Instructions:

1. Prepare vegetables and rinse them thoroughly.

2. Then cut celery, cucumber, and ginger into quarters.

3. Place juicer collector under the juicer's nozzle, switch it on and process all the ingredients until thoroughly juiced.

4. Pour the juice into a chilled glass and serve straight away.

Zucchini Juice

Whenever you're looking for a healthy refreshment, zucchini juice is ready to go! Why not give zucchini juice a try instead of that fruit juice in your refrigerator? Here are some reasons why you should ditch the store-bought juices and make your zucchini juice. You'll save money, have less sugar, help the environment by cutting back on plastic packaging, and feel more satisfied.

Prep Time: 5 Minutes

Serves: 1

Ingredients:

- 1 large zucchini
- 1 green apple, cored
- 1 medium cucumber, peeled
- 1-inch piece of ginger, peeled
- 1 lemon, peeled and seeded
- 2 tablespoons avocado oil

Instructions:

1. Prepare vegetables and fruits and rinse them thoroughly.

2. Then cut apple, cucumber, and ginger into quarters.

3. Place juicer collector under the nozzle of juicer, switch it on and process all the ingredients until thoroughly juiced.

4. Add oil into the juice and stir well.

5. Pour the juice into a chilled serving glass and serve straight away.

Radish Juice

Radish juice is an excellent source of many nutrients, including fiber, folate, calcium, niacin, vitamin A, and vitamin C. Radishes are also considered a diuretic that can help detoxify the body and kickstart your metabolism. They're also rich in redox antioxidants which have been shown to reduce the risk of developing chronic diseases such as heart disease or cancer.

Prep Time: 5 Minutes

Serves: 1

Ingredients:

- 1 bunch of radishes
- 2 medium green apples, peeled and cored
- 2 stalks of celery
- 1 large beet, peeled
- 2 tablespoons avocado oil

Instructions:

1. Prepare vegetables and fruits and rinse them thoroughly.

2. Then cut radish, apple, and beets into quarters.

3. Place juicer collector under the nozzle of juicer, switch it on and process all the ingredients until thoroughly juiced.

4. Add oil into the juice and stir well.

5. Pour the juice into a chilled serving glass and serve straight away.

Spinach Juice

Spinach is one of the most nutrient-dense foods on Earth, but it's also not precisely famous for its delicious taste. So what happens when you blend this leafy green into a healthy drink? It turns out that spinach juice might be the best thing since sliced bread. But there's more to this healthful beverage than meets the eye.

Prep Time: 5 Minutes

Serves: 2

Ingredients:

- 2 cups chopped spinach
- 1 medium apple, cored and chopped
- 1 stalk of celery
- 1/2 of lime, peeled and seeded
- 4 tablespoons avocado oil
- 3/4 cup filtered water, chilled

Instructions:

1. Prepare vegetables and fruits and rinse them thoroughly.

2. Then cut apple and celery into quarters.

3. Place juicer collector under the juicer's nozzle, switch it on and process all the ingredients until thoroughly juiced.

4. Add oil into the prepared juice, pour in water, and stir well.

5. Pour the juice into chilled glasses and serve straight away.

Celery and Spinach Juice

A study conducted by the National Institute of Diabetes and Digestive and Kidney Diseases suggests that celery serves as an excellent place to start when looking for a juicing recipe that could potentially positively affect your health. This is because celery has unique compounds called phthalides, which have been demonstrated to help prevent cancer and reduce the risk of some cancers.

Prep Time: 5 Minutes

Serves: 1

Ingredients:

- ½ of green apple, seeded
- 1 medium cucumber, peeled
- 2 handful spinach
- 3 medium stalks of celery
- ½ of a lemon, seeded
- 2 tablespoons avocado oil

Instructions:

1. Prepare vegetables and rinse them thoroughly.

2. Then cut apple and apple into quarters.

3. Place juicer collector under the juicer's nozzle, switch it on and process all the ingredients until thoroughly juiced.

4. Add oil into the prepared juice and stir well.

5. Pour the juice into a chilled glass and serve straight away.

Swiss Chard Juice

Green juice is all the rage these days, and for a good reason. Juicing can provide a healthy boost for your immune system, fill you up with liquid to keep hunger at bay and even help you shed some weight.

Swiss chard contains vitamin K (potent anti-aging properties), antioxidants (offer protection against cancer), and potassium (aids in muscle contractions). It also has an impressive amount of fiber, calcium, and protein.

Prep Time: 5 Minutes

Serves: 1

Ingredients:

- 4 large Swiss chard leaves
- 1 bunch of celery
- 1 medium cucumber, peeled
- ½ bunch of cilantro
- 1-inch piece of ginger, peeled
- 1 lemon, peeled
- 1 lime, peeled
- 2 tablespoons avocado oil

Instructions:

1. Prepare vegetables by chopping them all and then rinse well.

2. Place juicer collector under the juicer's nozzle, switch it on and process all the ingredients until thoroughly juiced.

3. Add oil into prepared juice and stir well.

4. Pour the juice into a chilled glass and serve straight away.

Tomato Juice

It may be simple, but tomato juice is one of the most popular beverages in America. Research by Nielsen shows that about 24% of Americans drink fresh or bottled tomato juice each week. It is a popular beverage for more than just the U.S. Tomato juice is consumed in over 130 countries across the globe, making it one of the top three sparkling beverage types worldwide.

Prep Time: 5 Minutes

Serves: 1

Ingredients:

- 2 large tomatoes, cored
- 1 medium stalk of celery
- 1 medium cucumber, peeled
- ¼ cup parsley
- ½ teaspoon sea salt
- 1/8 teaspoon cayenne pepper
- 2 tablespoons avocado oil
- ½ cup crushed ice

Instructions:

1. Prepare vegetables and rinse them thoroughly.

2. Then cut cucumber and tomatoes into quarters.

3. Place juicer collector under the juicer's nozzle, switch it on and process all the ingredients until thoroughly juiced.

4. Add oil and ice into prepared juice and stir well.

5. Pour the juice into a chilled glass and serve straight away.

Cauliflower Juice

What is cauliflower juice? The name's not too delicious, but the idea behind it is. Cauliflower is packed with vitamin C and other beneficial nutrients.

Prep Time: 5 Minutes

Serves: 2

Ingredients:

- 1 medium head of cauliflower, cut into small florets
- ½ bunch of spinach leaves
- 1 medium green apple, peeled and seeded
- 1 pomegranate, seeds only
- 1-inch piece of ginger
- 4 tablespoons avocado oil

Instructions:

1. Prepare vegetables and fruits and rinse them thoroughly.

2. Then cut cauliflower into small florets and apples into quarters.

3. Place juicer collector under the nozzle of juicer, switch it on and process all the ingredients until thoroughly juiced.

4. Add oil into prepared juice and stir well.

5. Pour the juice into a chilled glass and serve straight away.

Celery and Parsley Juice

Celery and parsley juice is a refreshing drink that brings many benefits to your body. It improves your digestion, decreases blood sugar levels, and protects you from developing kidney stones. This mixture also cleans the colon, which can often lead to improved conditions in the digestive system. To prepare celery and parsley juice, you'll need two glasses of water for every one glass of celery and parsley juice that you want to prepare.

Prep Time: 5 Minutes

Serves: 1

Ingredients:

- 2 medium stalks of celery
- 3 leaves of Swiss chard
- ½ inch turmeric, peeled
- 1 handful of parsley
- 1 lime, peeled and seeded
- 2 tablespoons avocado oil

Instructions:

1. Prepare vegetables and rinse them thoroughly.

2. Place juicer collector under the nozzle of juicer, switch it on and process all the ingredients except for lemon and water until thoroughly juiced.

3. Add oil into prepared juice and stir well.

4. Pour the juice into a chilled glass and serve straight away.

Cucumber and Mint Juice

The two most important things to remember when making a cucumber and mint juice are the ratios of cucumber to mint and how long the juicer is running.

If you don't enjoy strong-tasting juices, then one or two slices of cucumbers per leaf of mint are perfect. If you prefer a more robust taste, add more cucumber slices or include other fruits such as apples, oranges, or lemons. You should also try freezing your fruit before juicing for a cold treat on a hot day.

Prep Time: 5 Minutes

Serves: 1

Ingredients:

- 4 medium stalks of celery
- ½ of a medium cucumber, peeled
- 1 handful of parsley
- 1 handful of mint
- ½ of a medium lemon, peeled
- 2 tablespoons avocado oil

Instructions:

1. Prepare vegetables and fruits and rinse them thoroughly.

2. Then, cut the cucumber into quarters.

3. Place juicer collector under the nozzle of juicer, switch it on and process all the ingredients until thoroughly juiced.

4. Add oil into prepared juice and stir well.

5. Pour the juice into a chilled glass and serve straight away.

Bell Pepper Juice

Bell Pepper Juice is an effortless and time-saving way to make fresh vegetable juice! It's a great way to get your body on track for the summer, as it's better than drinking down lemonade or an apple any time of year, but it also makes a great alternative to store-bought pre-made juices. All you need is 1 bell pepper and water.

Prep Time: 5 Minutes

Serves: 1

Ingredients:

- 1 medium cucumber, peeled
- 1 medium red bell pepper, cored
- ¼ of a medium head of romaine lettuce
- 1 handful of parsley
- 2 tablespoons avocado oil

Instructions:

1. Prepare vegetables and rinse them thoroughly.

2. Place juicer collector under the nozzle of juicer, switch it on and process all the ingredients until thoroughly juiced.

3. Add oil into prepared juice and stir well.

4. Pour the juice into a chilled glass and serve straight away.

Kale Juice

Kale has been getting a lot of hype recently for its health benefits. It's rich in vitamins and nutrients, and it's an easy way to get a serving of greens into your diet. But where do you buy your kale? Grocery stores offer only the leaves, so you'll end up paying more money for less nutrition.

Prep Time: 5 Minutes

Serves: 1

Ingredients:

- 3 leaves of kale, chopped
- 3 handfuls of spinach
- 4 medium stalks of celery
- 1 medium cucumber, peeled
- 2 tablespoons avocado oil

Instructions:

1. Prepare vegetables and rinse them thoroughly.

2. Place juicer collector under the nozzle of juicer, switch it on and process all the ingredients until thoroughly juiced.

3. Add oil into prepared juice and stir well.

4. Pour the juice into a chilled glass and serve straight away.

Winter Green Juice

Sometimes, it is easy to fall into the rut of your daily routine and forget how important healthful living can be for you. Many people have a difficult time incorporating exercise or healthy eating into their busy schedules. This is often an excuse for people to stop taking care of themselves altogether.

Prep Time: 5 Minutes

Serves: 1

Ingredients:

- 1 medium green apple, peeled and cored
- ½ of a medium cucumber
- 1/4 of a medium head of green cabbage
- 6 leaves of romaine lettuce
- 4 sprigs of fresh mint
- 1-inch piece of ginger
- 2 tablespoons avocado oil

Instructions:

1. Prepare vegetables and fruits and rinse them thoroughly.

2. Then cut apple and cucumber into quarters and slice the cabbage into wedges.

3. Place juicer collector under the nozzle of juicer, switch it on and process all the ingredients until thoroughly juiced.

4. Add oil into prepared juice and stir well.

5. Pour the juice into a chilled glass and serve straight away.

Chard Parsley Green Juice

"Parsley is a wonderful leafy green veggie that offers many health benefits (including detoxification and protection from cancer). It's packed with vitamins A, C, K, calcium, iron, and potassium. Plus, it's low in calories so that it won't add to your waistline.

Prep Time: 5 Minutes

Serves: 1

Ingredients:

- 1 medium green apple
- 2 oranges, peeled
- 1/2 of a medium cucumber, peeled
- 2 leaves of Swiss chard
- 10 parsley sprigs
- 2 tablespoons avocado oil

Instructions:

1. Prepare vegetables and fruits and rinse them thoroughly.

2. Then cut apple, orange, and cucumber into quarters.

3. Place juicer collector under the nozzle of juicer, switch it on and process all the ingredients until thoroughly juiced.

4. Add oil into prepared juice and stir well.

5. Pour the juice into a chilled glass and serve straight away.

Mango, Strawberry, and Banana Juice

The sweet fruits of summer are in season, which means you can enjoy them all the year-long, even during winter. But what if your goal is to make a juice that tastes like a tropical vacation for pennies?

How about mango, strawberry, and banana juice? All three fruits are rich in vitamins A and C, potassium, and fiber. They're great for energizing your body. Plus, they taste amazing! And with this easy recipe, you can avoid additives used by some fruit juice manufacturers.

Prep Time: 5 Minutes

Serves: 1

Ingredients:

- ½ cup of strawberries, whole
- ½ cup of bananas, sliced thinly
- ¼ cup of mango, thinly sliced
- ½ cup of low-fat yogurt
- Ground peanuts, for sprinkling

Instructions:

1. In a blender, add the banana slices, whole strawberries, thinly sliced mango, and low-fat yogurt.

2. Blend on the highest setting until smooth in consistency.

3. Pour into a chilled glass and serve immediately.

Broccoli, Cucumber and Kiwi Juice

Broccoli, Cucumber, and Kiwi Juice is a tasty and refreshing drink that sticks to your ribs and can be used for breakfast or as a snack.

This drink is very healthy for you. It has less sugar than most fruit drinks, but the benefits of this drink are found in the nutrients it offers. The juice contains Vitamins A, C, K, and many of the B vitamins.

Prep Time: 5 Minutes

Serves: 1

Ingredients:

- 1 kiwi, peeled and thinly sliced
- 2/3 cup of pineapple, cut into chunks
- 1/3 cup of cucumber, thinly sliced
- 1/3 cup of broccoli, chopped

Instructions:

1. Wash the kiwi, pineapple, cucumber, and broccoli thoroughly.

2. In a blender, add the pineapple chunks, sliced kiwi, sliced cucumber, and chopped broccoli.

3. Blend on the highest setting until smooth in consistency.

4. Pour into a chilled glass and serve immediately.

Mango and Green Tea Juice

You may have heard of the alleged benefits of green tea in weight loss and cancer prevention. But did you know that it can also help you build muscle? Green tea is so beneficial to developing muscle because it contains a high amount of epigallocatechin gallate, which allows your body to use amino acids more effectively so they can be broken down and built into larger protein molecules.

Prep Time: 3 Minutes

Serves: 1

Ingredients:

- 1 cup of mango, thinly sliced
- ½ cup of green tea, freshly brewed
- 1 Tbsp. of honey
- ½ cup of low-fat yogurt
- 1 cup of ice cubes

Instructions:

1. In a blender, add the sliced mango, brewed green tea, honey, ice cubes, and low-fat yogurt.

2. Blend on the highest setting until smooth in consistency.

3. Pour into a chilled glass and serve immediately.

Apple, Red Leaf Lettuce, and Cucumber Juice

Recent studies have shown that drinking apple, red leaf lettuce, and cucumber juice for a few weeks before you go on a diet can help to reduce your weight by as much as 8% in less than two weeks. The reason behind the success of this type of liquid diet is from the chemical composition of these vegetables, which are all able to perform diuretic functions. This means they increase how many water molecules are removed from your body when digested and flushed out through urination.

Prep Time: 5 Minutes

Serves: 1

Ingredients:

- 1 green apple, cored removed
- ½ of a lemon fruit
- 5 leaves of red leaf lettuce
- 1 cucumber, thinly sliced

Instructions:

1. Wash the green apple, lemon fruits, leaves of red leaf lettuce, and cucumber thoroughly.

2. Peel the lemon fruit and remove the seeds

3. Add green apple, lemon fruit, red leaf lettuce, and sliced cucumber in a blender.

4. Blend on the highest setting until smooth in consistency.

5. Pour into a chilled glass and serve immediately.

Cucumber, Kale and Spinach Juice

If you're looking to get a little more vegetables into your diet while still getting the benefits of juicing in a simple, quick, and easy way, then you'll find so much joy in this short and sweet article. With only seven ingredients plus water, this juice is sure to give you a boost of nutrients. Plus, it's so simple to throw together on demand!

Prep Time: 3 Minutes

Serves: 1

Ingredients:

- 2 cucumbers, whole
- ½ cup of kale
- ¼ cup of spinach
- ¼ cup of parsley, chopped
- ¼ cup of Swiss chard
- ½ a slice of lemon

Instructions:

1. Rinse the kale, spinach, chopped parsley, and Swiss chard thoroughly. Remove the steam. 2. Wash the cucumber thoroughly. Slice into 1 inch thick slices.

2. Remove the rind and seeds from the lemon. Slice into 1 inch thick slices.

3. In a blender, add the cucumbers, kale, spinach, chopped parsley, Swiss chard, and lemon slices.

4. Blend on the highest setting until smooth in consistency.

5. Pour into a chilled glass and serve immediately.

Sweet Potato, Bell Pepper, Beet and Carrot Juice

I try to eat clean and practice healthy habits so finding a juice recipe that gets me excited is tough. This juice can be made with the same ingredients you would find in your favorite salad or vegetable soup. It can also be mixed with water for an easy, refreshing drink to share with others when you're out and about.

Prep Time: 5 Minutes

Serves: 1

Ingredients:

- 2 red apples, core removed
- 2 beets, sliced into wedges
- 1 cup of sweet potatoes, cut into cubes
- 1 red bell pepper, seeds removed and thinly sliced
- 1 carrot, peeled and thinly sliced

Instructions:

1. Wash the red apples, beet, sweet potatoes, red bell pepper, and carrots thoroughly.

2. In a blender, add the apples, beet wedges, sweet potato cubes, sliced red bell pepper, and sliced carrots.

3. Blend on the highest setting until smooth in consistency.

4. Pour into a chilled glass and serve immediately.

Asparagus, Coriander, and Onion Juice

Asparagus, coriander, and onion juice are a surprisingly great way to help reduce the hunger pangs, especially when combined with a light salad. Asparagus, coriander, and onion juice should be consumed in place of your usual food to avoid missing out on any nutrients. This meal will leave you feeling satisfied for hours on end.

Prep Time: 5 Minutes

Serves: 1

Ingredients:

- 1/3 cup of asparagus
- ½ cup of coriander leaves, chopped
- 1 ½ Tbsp. of white onion, chopped
- 2 Tbsp. of light brown sugar
- 1 ½ cup of water, distilled

Instructions:

1. Rinse the asparagus thoroughly. Cut into 1 inch thick cubes.

2. Place a saucepan over medium to high heat. Add in 2 cups of water. Add in the asparagus. Boil for 3 to 5 minutes or until bright green. Drain and pat dry.

3. Add the asparagus, chopped coriander leaves, chopped white, light brown sugar, and distilled water in a blender.

4. Blend on the highest setting until smooth in consistency.

5. Pour into a chilled glass and serve immediately.

Avocado, Spinach, and Lime Juice

This recipe is an easy, healthy way to eat your avocado and enjoy the added health benefits of spinach.

The lime juice adds a nice zing to the dish- try adding it in place of lemon juice or on top. The dressing can be drizzled over salads or used as a dip for pita breads.

Prep Time: 5 Minutes

Serves: 1

Ingredients:

- 1 1/3 cup of avocado, cut into cubes
- 2/3 cup of grapes, seedless
- 2 apples, core removed
- 2 cups of spinach leaves
- 3 stalks of celery, chopped
- 1 lime fruit, cut into pieces

Instructions:

1. Wash the avocado, seedless grapes, apple, spinach leaves, chopped celery, and lime fruit thoroughly.

2. Slice the avocado into halves and remove the seed.

3. Peel the lime and remove the seeds.

4. In a blender, add the apples, seedless grapes, avocado cubes, spinach leaves, and chopped stalks of celery and lime fruit pieces.

5. Blend on the highest setting until smooth in consistency.

6. Pour into a chilled glass and serve immediately.

Spinach, Carrot, and Watercress Juice

Healthy juice is more than just fruit and veg and isn't that hard to make. Try this spinach, carrot, and watercress juice for a refreshing, healthful drink.

There are plenty of delicious combinations to choose from when it comes to juicing, but none are more effective at fighting free radicals than spinach, carrot, and watercress juice. Rich in carotenoids that help fight cancer and antioxidants like vitamin A, C, and E, this is surely the perfect way to start your day.

Prep Time: 3 Minutes

Serves: 1

Ingredients:

- 2 carrots
- 1 cup of watercress
- ½ cup of spinach leaves, chopped
- ¼ cup of coriander leaves
- 2 tomatoes, whole

Instructions:

1. Rinse the carrots thoroughly. Chop into 1-inch sized cubes.

2. Rinse the watercress, chopped spinach leaves, and coriander leaves. Chop into small pieces.

3. Add carrot pieces, watercress, chopped spinach, coriander leaves, and whole tomatoes in a blender.

4. Blend on the highest setting until smooth in consistency.

5. Pour into a chilled glass and serve immediately.

Conclusion

The health benefits of juicing are many, but they can be lost if you aren't mindful of what you put into it. One of the most important things to pay attention to is what makes up the juice recipes.

Thank you for downloading this book.

About the Author

Ivy's mission is to share her recipes with the world. Even though she is not a professional cook she has always had that flair toward cooking. Her hands create magic. She can make even the simplest recipe tastes superb. Everyone who has tried her food has astounding their compliments was what made her think about writing recipes.

She wanted everyone to have a taste of her creations aside from close family and friends. So, deciding to write recipes was her winning decision. She isn't interested in popularity, but how many people have her recipes reached and touched people. Each recipe in her cookbooks is special and has a special meaning in her life. This means that each recipe is created with attention and love. Every ingredient carefully picked, every combination tried and tested.

Her mission started on her birthday about 9 years ago, when her guests couldn't stop prizing the food on the table. The next thing she did was organizing an event where chefs from restaurants were tasting her recipes. This event gave her the courage to start spreading her recipes.

She has written many cookbooks and she is still working on more. There is no end in the art of cooking; all you need is inspiration, love, and dedication.

Author's Afterthoughts

I am thankful for downloading this book and taking the time to read it. I know that you have learned a lot and you had a great time reading it. Writing books is the best way to share the skills I have with your and the best tips too.

I know that there are many books and choosing my book is amazing. I am thankful that you stopped and took time to decide. You made a great decision and I am sure that you enjoyed it.

I will be even happier if you provide honest feedback about my book. Feedbacks helped by growing and they still do. They help me to choose better content and new ideas. So, maybe your feedback can trigger an idea for my next book.

Thank you again

Sincerely

Ivy Hope

Made in the USA
Las Vegas, NV
07 July 2022

51220600R00066